decorating eggs

decorating eggs

15 fun and stylish projects
for decorating eggs

Deborah Schneebeli-Morrell

CICO BOOKS
LONDON NEW YORK

For Luna Schneebeli,
the light in our lives

Published in 2008 by CICO Books
an imprint of Ryland Peters & Small
519 Broadway, 5th Floor, New York, NY 10012

www.cicobooks.co.uk

10 9 8 7 6 5 4 3 2 1

A CIP catalog record for this book is available from the
Library of Congress

ISBN-13: 978 1 906094 28 7
ISBN-10: 1 906094 28 4

Printed in China

Editor: Gillian Haslam
Designer: Christine Wood
Illustrator: Trina Dalziel
Photographer: Heini Schneebeli
Stylist: Deborah Schneebeli-Morrell

contents

introduction

Of all the forms in nature, the egg must be the most beautiful with its perfect symmetry and infinite variety of subtle tones and colors. These so often match the coloring of the bird or fowl that laid them—the matte white shell of the goose egg echoes the snowy feathers on the bird itself, the tiny speckled guinea fowl's eggs remind us of the spotty patterned creatures, and everybody knows that brown hens lay brown eggs!

In many cultures the egg, which is so strongly associated with spring, has become a universal symbol of new life. It is, of course, a container of new life and all the potential it carries within. In Christian countries we give eggs at Easter as gifts, a throwback to pagan times when the egg may have been a potent ritual object. We have perhaps lost sight of the historic significance of this giving—we have come to expect chocolate Easter eggs, the finest being classic examples of the confectioner's art, but often they are expensive factory-made indulgences. How much better to revive some of the traditions of egg decorating. These enduring crafts are still practised in many countries, particularly in Europe where competitions are often held and supreme egg-decorating champions are chosen.

Below: *See page 60 for easy instructions for decorating goose eggs with traditional papercuts.*

This book will encourage you to try some traditional methods of decorating the egg, such as the scraffito project or the goose eggs with the papercut design, as well as encouraging you to be original and inventive. Some of the projects are ideal to make with children—the humorous cress heads are fun and the wooden egg alphabet game is easy to make as well as being an educational toy. There is even a project to entice the chocoholics!

You'll discover that eggs are wonderful to decorate. You can segment and divide the shape, creating facets to decorate. You can use the shell color as part of your design or cover it with fabric and braids. The possibilities are endless, but remember to be sensitive to the form—follow it, take it as your inspiration, and don't overwhelm it with too much color or pattern.

Because many of the projects use blown eggs, they will endure. Nothing looks nicer than a bowl of hand-decorated eggs and receiving one as an Easter gift will always outshine the shop-bought chocolate variety. With experience and by developing your skills, you will find yourself able to invent and create new ideas for decorating eggs.

basic equipment

There really is very little that you will need to buy in the way of specialist equipment or tools to make most of the projects in this book—this is one of the joys of decorating eggs as a hobby.

If you are one of those people who love to collect and hoard ephemera, old wrapping paper and cards, stamps, letters, magazines, scraps of ribbon and braid, small remnants of fabric, odd beads and buttons, or even dried flowers, then you will be well equipped to start making projects in this book. And don't forget that the main "ingredient" for these projects—the egg itself—can be bought from the supermarket or local store, or if you live in the country, see what is available at local farm shops.

Many of the projects use blown eggs—this means that a tiny hole has been made in one end of the shell so that the contents can be drained out. The advantage of blowing the egg is that with careful handling, the shell will last forever. You will find it useful to buy an egg-blowing kit. The kit can be purchased from mail-order craft suppliers (see page 64), and comprises a small drill and a very clever little hand-operated pump. The advantage of using this little pump is that you do not need to 'blow' the egg yourself, thus avoiding your lips coming into contact with raw egg which would concern some people. More importantly, you will only need to make one hole in the shell as the contents are blown out by pumping air into the cavity. See pages 10—11 for egg-blowing instructions.

Most other equipment listed for each project mainly consists of everyday craft tools and materials, all easily accessible and inexpensive. You will need a craft knife (choose one with a retractable blade for safety reasons) and small sharp scissors, paintbrushes, pencils, crayons, and paints. Masking fluid is used for the latex resist eggs on page 48. The gold leaf used on the monogrammed eggs on page 20 is used in such a small quantity that it will not cost much.

Other useful bits and pieces will be found in the sewing box, such as scraps of fabric, beads, thread, needles and ribbons. Similarly, small scraps of decorated and colored paper leftover from other projects will come in useful for the paper collage eggs.

Below: *These fabric-covered eggs, featured on page 40, demonstrate that you only need the smallest scraps of fabric to create these "jewels."*

types of eggs

As well as the many different colors and sizes of eggs laid by all types of fowl, craft stores and mail-order outlets sell eggs made of materials such as wood and polystyrene. Here's a guide to the different types of eggs.

Hen's eggs come in a wide variety of sizes as well as a subtle range of colors. Each type or breed of hen produces a characteristic egg. Consumers traditionally liked white-shelled eggs but more recently people have mistakenly thought that brown eggs are best, so it is now quite difficult to find pale or white eggs unless you buy direct from a farm or a specialist shop. Some rare breeds produce lovely pastel-colored eggs.

Duck eggs are mostly white with thicker shells, although they can be a blue shade, hence the description "duck-egg blue." These are lovely to work with as the shells are strong and less likely to crack.

Quail's eggs are the most delicate eggs with the softest shell, and their fragility means they can be difficult to use in craftwork. Highly patterned in their natural state with random, splattered coloring, they need no other decoration. It is best to use them as miniature design elements, as a table display which can be eaten, or carefully threaded onto a small garland.

Below: *Pure white duck and hen's eggs.*

Below right: *Tiny speckled quail's eggs.*

Goose eggs are exquisite. Pure white, elongated and with strong shells, they are perfect for decorative projects as they are so durable. They take color well and provide a beautiful matte surface for many types of design. These are prized eggs and are, of course, more expensive, but they are becoming more widely available.

Pheasant eggs are laid in loosely-made nests on the ground in long grass or field crops. Anyone who has discovered such a nest will marvel at the clutch of khaki-colored, slightly pointed eggs nestling in the center. They are, of course, available in the countryside but with the rise of farmers' markets, it is increasingly easy to find them in towns. Good supermarkets sometimes stock them.

Wooden eggs last forever. They are very adaptable for collage or painting. They are available in a wide variety of sizes from hobby or craft suppliers.

Papier-mâché eggs, especially the ones that split into two halves, are often decorated with a decoupage design. They are ideal for filling with small edible chocolate eggs and toys as an Easter present for young children.

Polystyrene eggs come in a variety of sizes and are available from hobby suppliers. They are ideal for projects where the whole egg is covered, especially where sewing or beading is involved. They are light and can be used as hanging decorations.

Below left: *Goose and pheasant's eggs.*

Below: *Wooden eggs and papier-mâché shells.*

blowing eggs

To blow eggs without the aid of an egg-blowing kit (see page 7), make two holes, one at each end of the egg, using the pointed blade of a small pair of scissors. Put one hole to your mouth and blow the contents out into a bowl.

Using an egg pump is much easier, especially if you want to blow many eggs.

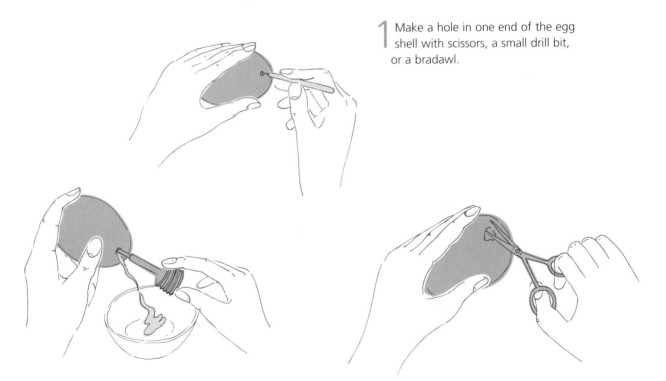

1 Make a hole in one end of the egg shell with scissors, a small drill bit, or a bradawl.

2 Insert the pump into the hole and pump air in carefully, allowing the egg contents to flow out of the same hole into a bowl placed below the egg.

3 If you want to enlarge the hole, carefully cut around the opening with a small pair of pointed scissors. This will be necessary if you want to thread the eggs onto wire or ribbon.

dyeing eggs

Always follow the manufacturer's instructions when using synthetic egg dye. Natural dyes are mixed with water and heated in a stainless steel pan. When dyeing blown eggs, you will need to fill the egg with some of the dye using the syringe so that the eggs are weighted and therefore fully immersed.

You can dry dyed eggs in a cardboard egg box, or on folded kitchen paper. If you are painting the eggs and the hole is sufficiently large, they can be threaded onto a chopstick and stood in a large glass or jug to dry.

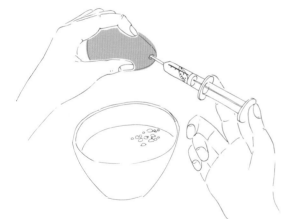

4 It is a good idea to wash eggs before decorating them. Fill them with warm soapy water using a syringe, then hold your finger over the hole, shake and rinse.

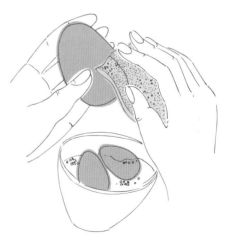

5 Clean the outside of the shell with a soft scouring sponge. Always make sure that the eggs are thoroughly dry inside and out before decorating them.

scraffito eggs

'Scraffito' literally means to scratch through, and it is a commonly used technique for decorating ceramics where a slip or top coating of color is scratched away to reveal the color beneath. This is a very popular method of decorating eggs in Switzerland where annual competitions are held. It is best to use duck eggs as their shells are much stronger, although you can use free-range or organic pale-colored hen's eggs.

you will need

▶ Old saucepan or bowl
▶ Easter egg dyes in red, green, and blue
▶ Slotted spoon
▶ Strong white duck or hen's eggs, blown (see page 10)
▶ Oval stencil
▶ White chinagraph pencil
▶ Craft knife

1 Dissolve the red dye in boiling water in an old saucepan or bowl, according to the instructions on the packet. Lower the eggs into the dye and leave for at least 10 minutes to take up the color. Cool slightly and remove from the dye. Allow to cool thoroughly.

Right: *Flower designs are traditional, effective, and simple to create. Cross-hatching, feathering and stars are the easiest motifs to create.*

top tip

There is a wide variety of synthetic egg dyes available and these are easy to use. Natural dyes produce subtler colors, but you will need to simmer the egg for longer to achieve the depth of color.

2 Lay the oval stencil over each side of the egg and mark the oval outline with the white chinagraph pencil. Next, draw a freehand line dissecting the egg in half lengthwise.

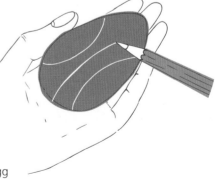

top tip
It is easiest to scratch the design on a boiled egg as you have to exert some pressure. Obviously a blown egg will be more durable, but you will need to use extra care when creating the scraffito design.

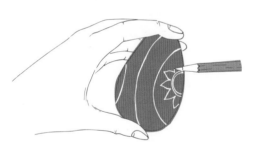

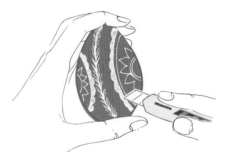

3 Draw your chosen design onto the egg using the white pencil—here I have drawn a flower within the oval outline and a scalloped edge around it. You don't need to mark all the elements—leave some to scratch freehand with the craft knife.

4 Using the craft knife, scratch along the white lines, gently but firmly removing the dye and revealing the natural color of the eggshell beneath. Start with the central line dividing the egg in two, then add a feathering on either side. Scratch the dye completely away from the scalloped oval border.

5 Scratch away the flower design, changing the pressure you apply to the craft knife to graduate the tone on the petals so they are lighter toward the center of the flower. Finally, create a trellis design in the center of the flower.

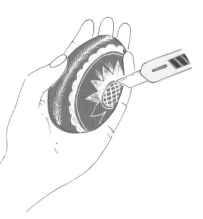

VARIATION (right)
These subtle earth-brown eggs have been dyed with natural dyes, in this case, redwood over pale hen's eggs. Images from the natural world have been used—a friendly bird in a cameo on one and stylized daisies on a banded egg on the other. These eggs have been blown so they will last forever.

quail's egg wreath

These exquisite speckled quail's eggs have been threaded alternately with pretty Indian rice-paper flowers and sprays of dried mimosa to make this beautiful wreath. It will last forever and can be brought out each Easter to hang on the front door of the house. All kinds of eggs lend themselves to wreaths—perhaps it is the suggestion of the shape of a nest that makes it seem obvious to thread them into a circle.

you will need

▶ Florist's wire, medium thickness
▶ Scissors
▶ 8 quail's eggs, blown (see page 10)
▶ 8 ready-made paper flowers (these are Indian rice-paper flowers, probably used in wedding garlands)
▶ Bunch of dried mimosa flowers (see Top Tip on page 18)
▶ Craft glue
▶ Yellow ribbon, for hanging

1 Cut a 24-in. length of the florist's wire. Thread on all the blown eggs and twist the wire ends together to form a circle.

2 Cut a 6-in. length of wire. Turn over one end and thread through the center of one of the rice-paper flowers. Place a flower between two eggs and bind the wire around the circle to secure. Do not cut off the ends of the wire. Repeat with the remaining flowers.

Right: *This beautiful wreath can be used to decorate the house at Eastertime. After the celebrations, carefully pack the wreath between layers of tissue paper in a sturdy cardboard box.*

3 Break off some mimosa sprays and arrange them around the flowers, making sure they all flow in one direction. Push some sprays into the hole at one end of each egg and secure with a dab of glue.

4 Bind the mimosa flower sprays in place on the wreath with the remaining wire flower stem, then cut off the excess wire. Add a tiny drop of glue as you go to fix everything in place.

5 Continue working around the wreath, adding mimosa sprays as you go. When complete, turn the wreath over gently and carefully add glue to all the loose stems, making sure you apply some to the holes in the eggshells. Allow the glue to dry. Turn over and attach a decorative yellow ribbon to the top of the wreath to allow you to hang it.

monogrammed hen's eggs

These stylish and elegant brown hen's eggs have been decorated with a single letter picked out in gold transfer leaf. This mysterious and ancient technique is surprisingly easy to achieve. To create the raised or embossed letter, simply paint the area to be gilded with two layers of craft glue.

you will need

▶ Letter template (see Top Tip)
▶ Scissors
▶ Brown hen's eggs, blown (see page 10)
▶ Craft glue
▶ White chinagraph pencil
▶ Fine paintbrush
▶ Gold size
▶ Transfer gold leaf
▶ Soft brush

1 Trace and cut out a letter template from a newspaper or magazine, or reduce or enlarge by photocopying to fit your chosen egg. Place onto the egg, holding in place with a small dab of glue on the back. Draw around the shape with the white pencil.

top tip

Look closely at newspapers and magazines—you will find many examples of different typefaces. Cut out and keep an assortment of styles so that you can use them as templates for the monogrammed letters.

Right: *Ordinary hen's eggs are turned into something very special by marking each shell with an elegant gold monogram.*

2 Remove the letter and paint carefully inside the white lines with the craft glue. Allow to dry, then recoat a second time to create the raised effect. Once again, allow to dry.

3 Paint the raised letter shape very neatly with the gold size. It is easy to see where you are painting as it is a milky color. Allow to dry—gold size always remains slightly tacky.

top tip
In order to keep the eggs indefinitely, use blown ones. You could, however, decorate hard-boiled eggs for a special occasion, such as a celebratory picnic or for stunning placements for an Easter meal.

4 Cut out a piece of gold transfer leaf large enough to cover over the whole letter. Press very firmly to transfer the leaf onto the tacky size. Gently remove the paper, leaving the gold in place. Tidy up by brushing away excess gold leaf with the soft brush—it will only stick where it is in contact with the gold size.

cress heads

This is definitely the most amusing project in the book, simple to make and practical too. Cress seeds grow quickly, the spicy flavor adding a perfect and traditional addition to egg sandwiches. The green seedlings are cress and the red ones are beet. The hole at one end of the egg has been enlarged with a small pair of scissors to make it large enough for planting seeds.

you will need

- Small pointed scissors
- Assortment of blown eggs
- Pencil
- Acrylic paint in dark brown, orange, pink, and ocher
- Pointed paintbrush
- Peat-free compost
- Teaspoon
- Sprouting seeds: rocket, cress or beet

1 Using small scissors, carefully insert them in the hole at one end of the egg and cut around it—it needs to be large enough to spoon in the compost.

2 Lightly draw faces onto each egg in pencil. Follow the expressions shown here to create a gallery of faces.

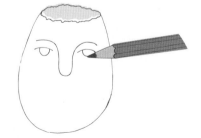

3 Neatly add the eyes, nose and mouth to the egg, using brown paint.

4 Paint small circles of pink, orange, or ocher to represent the cheeks.

5 Spoon the compost into the shells, to within ⅜in. of the top edge. Dampen the compost with a small drop of water.

6 Sprinkle the seeds onto the damp compost and wait two or three days for the seedlings to appear.

top tip
Water sparingly. It is very important that the compost stays fresh otherwise the seeds may go moldy and fail to germinate.

Right: *Experiment with different seed varieties. Choose the varied leaf shapes and colors to match the assortment of egg types. Sprouting seeds are available from good seed suppliers.*

braided eggs

One of the most striking aspects of eggs is the variety of natural colors that appear in the shells. The subtle, pastel blue eggs used here are from a rare breed of chicken called Old Cotswold Legbar. Use these beautiful qualities as part of your design, in this case allowing the segments of egg to show through the strips of braid.

you will need

▶ Pastel-colored eggs, blown (see page 10)
▶ Small pointed scissors
▶ Craft glue
▶ Small paintbrush
▶ 20-in. lengths of braid (here I've used pink cross-grain with brown spots, pink, and green looped silk)
▶ Small knitting needle

1 Open up the hole at the end of the egg with the points of the scissors to make it very slightly larger (just large enough to hold the ends of the ribbon). Paint a very light line of glue lengthwise around the egg.

Right: Make a group of eggs using a selection of different braids. They are so quick to make and there are so many ribbons and braids available from good sewing outlets. Try gingham and rickrack or chiffon with daisy chains.

2 Cut a length of the pink braid to reach around this line, leaving a tail of ½in. at each end. Lay the braid on the glue line and press gently into place. Dab some glue into the blow hole, then tuck each end of the braid into the hole using the knitting needle or the point of the scissors.

3 Paint on another line of glue and add a second length of the pink braid, dissecting the egg into quarters. Tuck the ends into the hole very carefully—the shell is most fragile at this point.

4 Glue on the narrower silk braid in the same way, dissecting the egg into eight segments. As before, tuck the ends of the braid into the hole, carefully adding a small dab of glue to secure.

Right: *This egg has been decorated with a contrasting green cross-grain ribbon, intersected by a pretty mauve woven braid. This project is ideal for using up small leftover lengths of ribbon.*

Below: *All the ribbon and braid colors are chosen carefully to complement the pastel shell.*

felted wool egg cozies

These charming egg cozies are simple to make, and you need only scraps of felted wool. Choose your colors carefully and use simple wool embroidery stitches to decorate your cozy. They are lined with a softer finely knitted fabric to give an extra layer of insulation.

you will need

▶ Paper and pencil
▶ Scissors
▶ Scraps of colored felted wool in pink, orange, and green
▶ Old felted sweater, for the lining (see Top Tip on page 32)
▶ Crewel wool in pink, yellow, and orange
▶ Yellow button
▶ Tapestry needle

1 Draw a template for the chicken head egg cozy on paper, making sure it will be large enough to slip over the egg. Also draw a template for the comb. Cut out the templates. Lay the template of the head onto the felted wool and pin in place. Cut out two heads from the felted wool and a further two from the felted sweater (this will form the lining). Cut out one comb from the orange felted wool.

2 Cut out a small felt circle for the eye. Stitch in place using radiating stitches in crewel wool to form the eye. Stitch the yellow button in place on top of the circle.

Right: *These jolly felted wool cozies will keep your breakfast eggs at just the right temperature.*

3 Create the decorative lines along the beak and neck using stem stitch and a contrasting color of crewel wool.

top tip
Old blankets or worn-out sweaters are ideal for this project. Wash them on a very hot cycle in the washing machine to felt them. They can also be dyed in the washing machine.

4 Put all layers of the cozy together, with the lining sandwiched between the two outer pieces of felted wool. Pin the comb between the lining at the top of the head. Stitch all four thicknesses together around the sides and top using blanket stitch. At the base, make the opening by stitching the outer pink layer to the mauve lining on each side. Over-stitch the edges of the comb with the same thread.

VARIATION (above)
This strikingly modern design, using scraps of felted wool and assorted buttons with simple embroidery, is quick and easy to make. The edge is bordered with a thick red chenille thread which is cleverly looped at the top. This design would lend itself readily to making a matching cozy for a coffee pot.

engraved duck eggs

Duck eggs have a beautiful matte white texture which lends itself wonderfully to this restrained decoupage technique where only a section of the egg is covered. As the eggs are blown and the shells are strong, these lovely objects with their classic design will last forever. They look stunning displayed in a white porcelain bowl, echoing the monochrome theme.

you will need

- Selection of antique engravings
- Plastic oval template
- Pencil
- Small sharp scissors
- Bowl of water
- Kitchen paper
- Craft glue
- Paintbrush
- White duck eggs, blown (see page 10)
- Black permanent marker, medium tip

1 Choose your engraving and lay the plastic template over the chosen section. You will need to choose the size of the oval opening to fit the egg, leaving enough room for the permanent marker decoration. Draw neatly inside the oval with the pencil.

top tip
Antique engravings can often be found in flea markets and antique shops.

2 Cut out the marked oval with the scissors. Mark and cut out another oval for the other side of the egg.

Right: *Using the theme of a house for the images gives a cohesion to the display. You may like to use animals or portraits— take your inspiration from the subjects you find amongst the engravings.*

3 Put the engravings into a bowl of water and soak until soft and flexible (but not until they become so soft that the paper tears). Remove and pat dry with kitchen paper. Paint a thin layer of glue on the back of the paper, then lay it glue side down centrally onto the long side of the egg, gently smoothing out any creases with your fingers. The moist paper should make this easier. Stick the second engraving in place on the other side of the egg.

4 Allow the paper to dry thoroughly. Using the black marker pen, draw a line ⅛in. away from each of the oval images. Next, draw a frame of freehand loops around this line as a decorative border to the engraved image. Finally, draw a straight line dissecting the egg lengthwise and making a central division to the design.

top tip
If the paper creases will not smooth out, carefully cut two darts on each side of the image. These will come together over the concave surface of the egg. It is easier to cut the darts before the paper is moistened.

easter egg garland

One can easily be tempted to over-complicate when decorating eggs. The egg shape is the most perfect in nature and here is a project that celebrates and recognizes that perfection. A small variety of pure undecorated eggs are simply threaded on a double chiffon knotted ribbon. Add a few more eggs to make a longer garland that threads around an Easter table or suspend a shorter length from a garden tree with spring blossom.

Below: This silk ribbon is very soft and settles beautifully when tied into a knot or bow. It is important to match the delicacy and fragility of the eggs with a suitable ribbon.

you will need

- Small pointed scissors
- Gimlet
- 3 hen's eggs with brown and ivory shells, blown (see page 10)
- 2 pheasant's eggs, blown
- 1 white duck egg, blown
- 2 pastel eggs (such as Old Cotswold Legbar), blown
- 3-yard lengths of chiffon ribbon in blue and brown
- Long needle with large eye (such as a mattress needle)

1 Using the points of the scissors, slightly enlarge the holes in the eggs so they are just large enough to accommodate the ribbon. Use the gimlet to push a hole in the other end of each egg, then enlarge slightly with the points of the scissors.

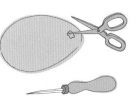

2 Lay the two lengths of ribbon side by side and thread together through the needle. Direct the needle through the first hen's egg.

3 Pull the ribbons through, leaving 6in. at the end. Tie a knot in the ribbon to secure the egg. Tie a further knot at the other side of the first egg before threading the second egg. Pull the eggs together tying a loose knot after each one. Thread the eggs in any order you wish, but make sure you alternate sizes and colors.

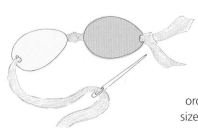

top tip
It is important to choose the ribbon color carefully to avoid overwhelming the subtle and delicate colors of the eggs themselves.

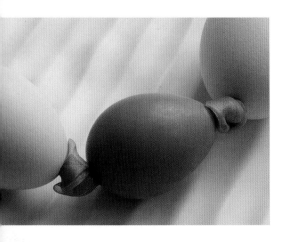

4 Continue threading and knotting the eggs until all are in place. Tie a final knot and trim the ends of the two ribbons diagonally to prevent fraying.

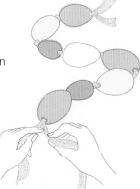

VARIATION (right)
This charming little
garland of quail's eggs has
been threaded in the same
way onto a dip-dyed silk
ribbon. It makes a pretty
and unusual surround for
a scented candle, but
would also look lovely
hanging over the side of
a dressing table mirror or
as a decorative wreath
on a cupboard door.

fabric-covered eggs

The egg shape is so perfect that it is copied in many materials. Here polystyrene eggs make a brilliant base for a more sumptuous form of decorating. Because it is soft and yielding, polystyrene can be pierced and pinned, lending itself to more complicated forms of embellishment. You will only need small scraps of fabric, braid, and ribbon and very simple sewing skills. A small collection of such eggs looks beautiful suspended from a silk ribbon threaded with matching beads.

you will need

▶ Polystyrene eggs in assorted sizes
▶ Scraps of fabric, such as Chinese silk with woven flower motif, fine printed cotton, etc.
▶ Scissors
▶ Pins
▶ Needle and white thread
▶ Selection of 20-in. lengths of ribbon in different widths, such as turquoise silk, purple taffeta, shot green rayon, etc.
▶ Assorted woven braids, such as green looped, chiffon flowerbuds, pink daisies, etc.
▶ Thread to match ribbons and braid
▶ Chenille needle
▶ Assorted glass beads

1 Cut a piece of fabric with a central woven motif slightly larger than half the egg shape. Lay the fabric over the egg and pin around the central line of the egg.

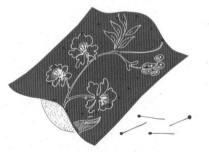

top tip
Polystyrene eggs are available from hobbycraft stores and mail-order craft websites.

2 Cut off the excess fabric just outside the line of pins. Cut a similar piece of fabric and pin in place on the other side of the egg, again cutting off the excess fabric.

Right and above: *Raid
your scrap bag for tiny
remnants of beautiful
fabric in jewel-like colors
and oddments of ribbons,
braids, and trimmings—
the smallest scraps can
transform these eggs
into treasures.*

3 Using the needle and white thread, sew the two sides of fabric together all around the join, pulling them to stretch the fabric as you sew. Fasten off firmly.

4 Cut a length of purple taffeta ribbon to stretch around the join in the fabric, turn over a small hem at the overlap and sew in place using matching color thread. Sew the green looped braid along each edge of the ribbon, then sew the chiffon flowerbud braid centrally down the ribbon with invisible stitches.

5 Make a small rosette by folding a length of the rayon ribbon into 12 loops, securing each loop with a stitch to hold it in place. Thread the chenille needle with a double length of the turquoise silk ribbon and attach to the center of the narrow end of the egg in the center of the purple ribbon, leaving the two ends free. Tie a knot to secure and cut the ends, leaving tails of 1in.

6 Thread the silk through the rosette, following on with an assortment of green and purple beads. Tie a knot in the silk ribbon after the last bead, then tie another knot at the top for hanging the egg.

VARIATION (right)
This larger polystyrene egg is covered in a heavier patterned fabric. The hanging ribbon is threaded with small beads and felt flowers.

egg mobile

There is a kind of poetic irony in turning these weightless white eggs into birds which can fly! Allowing the eggs to float freely means you can fully appreciate the lovely natural shape. They need very little to adorn them—just a few cleverly cut and folded pieces of patterned paper make a clear suggestion of a plump bird. You could use brightly colored feathers instead, although they are not so easy to attach seamlessly to the body of the bird.

you will need

- 4 small sheets of handmade patterned paper in purple, green, beige, and gray
- Scissors
- Craft glue
- Paintbrush
- 4 white duck eggs (or any large eggs), blown (see page 10)
- Pink beading cord
- Needle with large eye
- 4 small wooden beads and a small selection of other wooden beads for balancing
- 4 rubber bands
- 3 chopsticks
- Secateurs
- Small electric drill with tiny bit, ³⁄₁₆in.

1 Cut an oval shape from the green colored paper measuring roughly 1¼ x 1½in. Using craft glue, stick on the underside of the egg, toward the larger end to resemble the bird's breast.

top tip

This mobile is relatively easy to make and is a perfect project for an adult to create alongside a child. The actual hanging and balancing of the mobile is slightly more complicated, but working it out can be an enjoyable lesson in balance and weight.

Right: *Suspend your bird mobile in a place where it will catch the breeze, and the birds will appear to fly.*

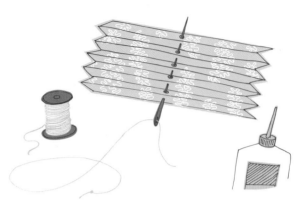

2 Cut out a 4 x 4in. square of matching paper to make the wings. Fold it into a concertina shape, each fold being roughly ½in. wide.

3 Cut a 6-in. length of the pink cord and thread through the needle. Tie a knot in the end and sew through all the folds in the center of the paper. While sewing, put a small dab of glue between each fold and one on the top.

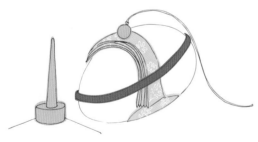

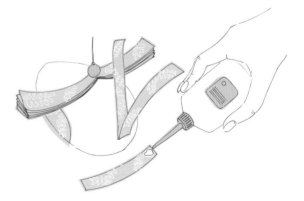

4 Thread on a wooden bead and tie a knot closely above it. Add a more generous dab of glue underneath the folds and place the wings on top of the egg, slightly toward the front. Keep the paper folded and secure gently to the egg with a rubber band until the glue is very firmly set (it is best to leave overnight). When dry, remove the rubber band and open out the wings.

5 To make the tail, cut tapered pieces of the same paper in varying lengths of 2½, 2¾ and 3½in. Stick the base of each strip over the blow hole at the back of the egg, overlapping them as you glue them.

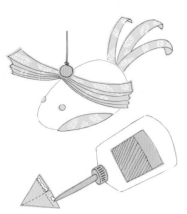

6 Cut two small paper circles for eyes and stick in place on each side of the egg in front of the wings. Fold another piece of paper and cut a triangle to make a beak shape. Snip one end of the fold and bend back the flaps, apply glue, and stick in place at the front of the bird. Allow the glue to dry thoroughly.

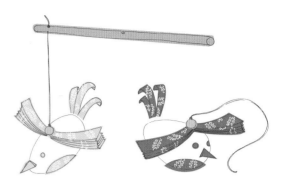

7 Make a further three similar birds using the other paper colors, each with the same length of cord attached. Using secateurs, cut the chopsticks to 8½in. in length. Drill three equidistant holes (one at each end and one in the middle) in each chopstick. Thread the cords attached to the eggs through the end holes and knot to secure.

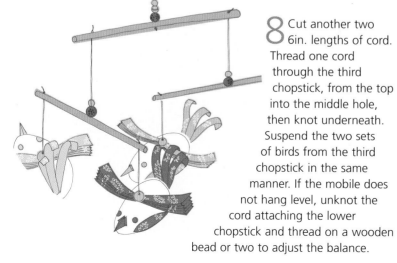

8 Cut another two 6in. lengths of cord. Thread one cord through the third chopstick, from the top into the middle hole, then knot underneath. Suspend the two sets of birds from the third chopstick in the same manner. If the mobile does not hang level, unknot the cord attaching the lower chopstick and thread on a wooden bead or two to adjust the balance.

latex resist eggs

This simple technique forms the basis of much decorative design, the idea being that you mask an area that you want to remain undecorated and simply paint or dye the rest in one go. When the paint is dry, just rub and pull off the masking fluid to reveal the pristine eggshell color beneath. There are intricate examples of this craft in egg decoration, particularly the many colored batik-painted eggs from the Czech Republic.

you will need

▶ Small pointed scissors
▶ White or blue duck eggs, blown (see page 10)
▶ Chopsticks
▶ Art masking fluid
▶ Acrylic paint in red, pink, and orange
▶ Paintbrush
▶ 1-yard length of two-tone ribbon in red/orange
▶ Crochet hook

1 Use the scissors to enlarge the hole at the end of the egg and make a new hole at the other end so that it is large enough to thread onto the double ribbon. Make sure that the eggs are really clean and dry and free from grease (wash if necessary and dry in a warm oven). Thread the chopstick into one hole to enable you to hold the egg, then paint a number of large spots all around the shell with the masking fluid.

Right: *The natural-colored resist pattern contrasts well against the brightly colored eggs.*

2 Paint a series of smaller dots around the larger circles, set aside, and allow the fluid to dry thoroughly.

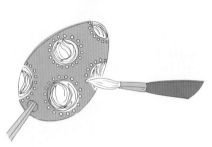

3 Mix the red paint with a little water until it flows smoothly, then paint the egg all over, including the masked areas. Leave to dry. Decorate the other eggs in the same way using different patterns and the pink and orange paints. When the paint is thoroughly dry, rub the areas painted with latex. It will pull off, coming away easily in an elastic fashion.

4 Fold the ribbon in half and push the fold through the first egg, pull gently through using the crochet hook from the other end. Tie a knot below the egg, leaving tails of 3¼in. Next, tie a knot above the egg and repeat for the other two eggs, tying knots above and below, leaving a hanging loop at the top.

VARIATION (right)
The subtler coloring on
these eggs is a simple
variation of the main
project. The eggs were
first dyed lilac and the
patterns were painted
with masking fluid. They
were then dyed again in
hot dye, each egg in blue,
yellow, or red. This has
removed the lilac tone
except where masked
and has left a subtle hint
of the secondary colors.
These techniques can
produce surprising and
unexpected effects.

chocolate eggs

It is not as difficult as you might think to make your own molded chocolate eggs as the techniques are very simple. Mauve and purple are the perfect color contrasts to the deep brown of rich dark chocolate and edible violet petals, with their characteristic floral fragrance, make the perfect decoration. Mauve-tinted royal icing piped in wavy lines around the egg completes the design.

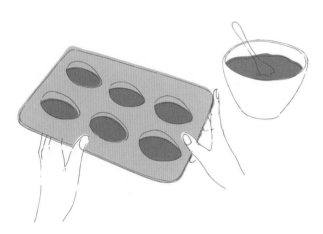

you will need

- 7oz dark chocolate, 70% solids
- Bain marie (heatproof glass bowl set over a small saucepan of hot water)
- 6-section plastic chocolate mold
- Sheet of baking parchment
- Cotton or plastic gloves (optional)
- Sharp knife
- Royal icing, tinted mauve with food coloring
- Piping bag and small decorative nozzle
- Crystallized violets

1 Break the chocolate up into small pieces and place in the bain marie over a low heat. As the chocolate melts, remove the bowl from the heat and cover until all the chocolate is fluid. Pour a spoonful into each clean mold, tip and rotate to allow the chocolate to cover the inside. Let the chocolate set, then add a couple more layers in the same manner until the chocolate shells are approximately ³⁄₁₆in. thick.

Right: *Home-made chocolate Easter eggs are fun to make and your efforts will mean a lot to the lucky recipient.*

2 Release the eggs over a clean sheet of baking parchment, spread a little melted chocolate around the rim as "glue" and close the two halves to secure. (You may like to wear plastic or cotton gloves to protect the chocolate from fingerprints.) Allow to set hard.

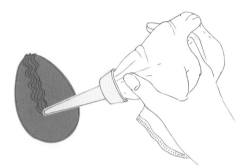

3 Trim the excess chocolate "glue" from the join with a sharp knife. Pour the mixed royal icing into the piping bag and pipe a wavy line all around the egg, dissecting it lengthwise. Pipe another line intersecting the first in the same way, dividing the egg into four sections. You will have to do this line in two parts, allowing one to dry hard before turning the egg over to pipe the other side.

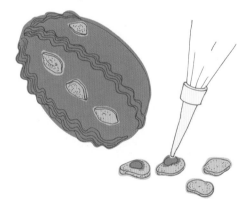

4 Add a dab of icing on the back of each violet petal and stick onto the chocolate in rows of three in each of the four sections. Keep the decorated eggs in a cool place once made.

top tip
Wrapped in cellophane and tied with a pretty chiffon bow, the eggs will make a delicious Easter gift. If you wish, you could pipe the recipient's name or initial onto the egg.

papier-mâché eggs

Undecorated papier-mâché shells come in two halves that fit together to make a container. Available from hobby suppliers, they can be found in a variety of sizes and make a perfect form to decorate in a simple way. Here, the outside has been covered with pink and terra cotta origami paper and the inside has been covered with pages from an old wildflower book. They are an Easter tradition—fill them with small toys or chocolate eggs as a gift for children on Easter Sunday.

you will need

▶ Pages from a wildflower book, or other black-and-white images
▶ Small scissors
▶ Papier-mâché shells—I used eggs 3¼in. long for the main project
▶ Craft glue
▶ Paintbrush
▶ Origami paper in pink and terra cotta

Right: *The smaller egg with the wildflower paper decorating the outside of the shell is lined with the pink pages of an old French encyclopedia.*

1 Cut the wildflower images into pieces large enough to cover the inside of the egg shells. Spread a small amount of glue on the back and smooth into place, working out any creases or air bubbles with your fingers. Overlap each piece and bring it up and over the protruding lip. Just decorate the inside on the other half, not the lip.

2 Cover the outside of each of the shell halves in the same way using the pink origami paper. As before, use small, overlapping pieces.

3 Cut a strip of terra cotta paper ¼in. wide and paste around the rim tucking it in neatly against the protruding lip. Cut a wider strip of terra cotta paper and stick in place over the rim so that it makes a border on both the inside and the outside of the shell.

4 Cut a circle of the terra cotta paper approximately 1¾in. across. Use the small scissors to cut small slices out of the circle all the way around, but leave the center intact. Spread glue lightly on the back and place centrally onto the egg shell, smoothing out any folds with your fingers. Allow the glue to dry.

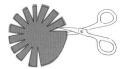

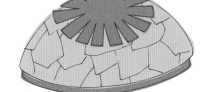

top tip
You can use any paper for this project as long as it is thin and flexible enough to cover the curved area of the shell without creasing. Using thicker paper would stop the shell from closing easily.

wooden egg alphabet game

In this project little wooden eggs are painted in pastel colors and letters in different colors and typefaces have been pasted onto one side. Fill a decorated papier-mâché shell (as shown on page 55) with them, along with a few chocolate candies, and make a surprising Easter gift for a child. If you can include enough different letters, it will lead to many hours of quiet entertainment spelling out names and words.

(as shown on page 55)

you will need

- Small wooden eggs, 1¾in. long
- Trial-size pots of emulsion paint, in pale pink, duck-egg blue, and taupe
- Paintbrush
- Craft glue
- Small-size assorted letters, gathered from books, magazines, packaging, etc.
- Small scissors

top tip
If you want the eggs to last and stay clean, you could finish them with a matte water-based varnish.

1 Divide the eggs into three groups and paint each group one of the three colors. You will need to given the eggs at least three coats of paint, allowing the paint to dry thoroughly between each coat. You may need to paint half the egg at a time so that you can hold it as you paint.

2 Assemble the letters and cut closely around them to isolate them from any other marks or images. Apply a small amount of glue to the back and place onto the front of the egg, smoothing out any creases and encouraging the paper to curve with the surface of the egg. Allow to dry, then pack into a decorated papier-mâché egg.

Above and right:
The papier-mâché shell, subtly lined with pink paper, has been covered on the exterior with larger sections of black-and-white type cut from newspapers, catalogs and sheet music. See pages 55—57 for instructions on making the papier-mâché shell.

papercut goose eggs

This simple, bold and colorful design is inspired by the Polish folk technique of papercutting. The main motif will bring back early memories for many people—it is a simple circle of colored paper folded into eight segments, then snipped at intervals along the fold lines to create a kind of snowflake we all made as children.

you will need

▶ Colored origami paper, including turquoise and brown
▶ Small scissors
▶ Pinking shears
▶ Craft glue
▶ Small paintbrush
▶ Goose eggs, blown (see page 10)

top tip

Only two colors of paper have been used on each egg as it is important not to disguise the beautiful shape and pure white qualities of the goose egg.

1 Cut a narrow strip of brown paper approximately ⅛in. wide and long enough to reach around the egg lengthwise (you may need to join two strips). Cut a wider strip of turquoise paper ½in. wide using the pinking shears to create a zigzagged edge on both sides. Using the glue, stick the turquoise strip in place on the egg, then stick the brown strip centrally on top. Smooth the paper with your fingers to mold it over the curved surface of the egg.

Right: *Papercutting is an easy craft to master, but the results are stunning.*

2 Cut out a circle from the brown paper 2½in. across (this measurement may vary according to the size of your egg). Fold it into eight segments by folding four times. Use the small scissors to cut a V shape out of the pointed end, then carefully cut small nicks in the folded sides, and zigzag the cut curved edge.

top tip
The paper used should be thin enough to stretch over the surface of the egg without creasing too much. Packs of smallish squares of colored paper used for origami are ideal.

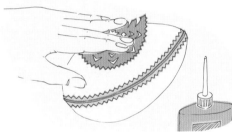

3 Open out the "snowflake" and lightly but evenly cover with the glue. Hold over the center of one half of the egg and press in place, smoothing out any folds as you press.

VARIATION (right)
These lovely white duck eggs have been decorated very simply by banding them with strips of patterned paper, old wallpaper, and wrapping paper. If you save and collect bits of decorated paper as you see them, you will always have a ready supply for a simple paper collage or decoupage project.

4 Cut out two smaller circles in the turquoise paper, approximately ⅝in. across. Make eight small nicks around the circumference, making sure the center is left intact. Stick in place, then cut a small dot of brown to glue in the center. Repeat the design on the other side of the egg.

suppliers

Panduro Hobby
Online craft supplies (including egg-blowing kit)
www.pandurohobby.com

Hobbycraft
Online craft supplies
www.hobbycraft.com

If you have any difficulty finding an egg-blowing kit,
just enter "egg blowing" or "egg blower" into an online
search engine to find suppliers.

acknowledgments

Many thanks to my publisher, Cindy Richards, for commissioning this book and
to Gillian Haslam for her seamless editing and constant encouragement. Thanks
to Christine Wood for the beautiful, simple design, and to Trina Dalziel for the
charming illustrations. I am, as ever, grateful to my husband, Heini Schneebeli,
for taking the lovely photographs in the book.